The Blue Peter Book of Odd Odes

The Blue Peter Book of Odd Odes

Edited by Biddy Baxter and Rosemary Gill
with illustrations by Peter Firmin

British Broadcasting Corporation

Published by the British Broadcasting Corporation
35 Marylebone High Street, London W1M 4AA

ISBN 0 563 17002 6

First published 1975

© British Broadcasting Corporation and the contributors 1975

Printed in England by Hazell Watson & Viney Ltd
Aylesbury, Bucks

Acknowledgements are due to the following for
permission to reproduce copyright material: J. M.
Dent and Sons Ltd for *The Canary, Reflection on Babies*
and *The Termite* from FAMILY REUNION by
Ogden Nash; Dobson Books Ltd for *On the Ning Nang
Nong* and *Look at all those Monkeys* from SILLY
VERSE FOR KIDS by Spike Milligan; Wolfe
Publishing for *Matilda Morgan* and *Willie Plank* from
CYRIL FLETCHER'S ODD ODES.

Introduction

My Odd Ode

This is an odd ode I tried to write
I tried and tried but it wouldn't go right.
All the lines were far too long,
And the rhyme kept going wrong.
I thought so hard I hurt my head,
I even tried to write in bed!
I try so hard to get it right,
And my fingers are clasping tight,
To my hot pen which is starting to grease,
The trouble is my fingers won't release,

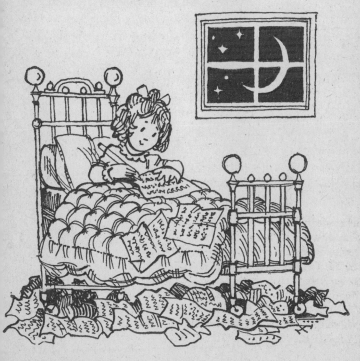

Until I have finished my very odd ode,
Which is turning out to be in my code!

Dear John, Pete and Lesley,

It is very hard work writing an odd ode. If it is possible could one of you make one up? I just want to see how *you* manage. It has taken me eight days to write one.

Love Claire

That was one of the eleven thousand five hundred and twenty-one entries for our Blue Peter Odd Odes Competition.

After our success with limericks, when thousands of viewers sent us their ideas and we were able to publish a whole book of them, we realised just how much people enjoy making up rhymes, and "Odd Odes" seem to bring out the most amazing ideas and flights of fancy. But ten-year-old Claire Hunt who lives in Hythe, Kent, wasn't the only one who found that making up the best rhymes and funny situations isn't always easy. Eleven-year-old Susan Allbut from West Buckland in Somerset, actually called *her* ode "Problem!"

I have tried to write an odd ode for you,
But it seems more than I can do,
I've got queer old aunts, in number six,
They're always getting in a fix,
Good subjects for an odd ode they,
But I can't do it – not today,
My father isn't a bad old sport,
My mum is a real good sort
They should be put into this rhyme,
To do it would take too much time
My budgie is a bright and noisy bird
My goldfish though is seldom heard
To write about them would be good,
And I would do it if I could,
This odd ode is a lot of trouble,
It's almost got me seeing double!

Someone else who found there was more to "Odd Ode" writing than meets the eye was Anita Johnston of Workington in Cumbria, and her nine-year-old brother Graeme made up an ode all about *her* problems:

This is the tale of my sister Anita,
Who thought she would write an odd ode for Blue Peter.
Her pen she discovered was right out of ink,
The only pencil around was a bright shocking pink.
However, she started to think up a rhyme,
"Good heavens," she said, "this will take a long time."
My sister Anita she thought and she thought,
And all that she had on her paper was nought.
She remembered the prizes she wanted to win,
But her mind was a blank and her head in a spin.
At last she gave up and ran off to bed,
So I sat down and wrote an odd ode instead.

Odd Odes were started by Cyril Fletcher in 1936 but for many years before that people had been writing comic verses.
This one was written some time between 1768 and 1826.

The Comic Adventures
of Old Mother Hubbard and Her Dog

Old Mother Hubbard
Went to the cupboard,
To give her poor dog a bone;
When she got there
The cupboard was bare,
And so the poor dog had none.

She went to the baker's
To buy him some bread;
When she came back
The dog was dead.

She went to the undertaker's
To buy him a coffin;
When she came back
The dog was laughing.

She took a clean dish
To get him some tripe;
When she came back
He was smoking his pipe.

She went to the hatter's
To buy him a hat;
When she came back
He was feeding the cat.

She went to the barber's
To buy him a wig;
When she came back
He was dancing a jig.

She went to the cobbler's
To buy him some shoes;
When she came back
He was reading the news.

She went to the seamstress
To buy him some linen;
When she came back
The dog was spinning.

She went to the hosier's
To buy him some hose;
When she came back
He was dressed in his clothes.

The dame made a curtsy,
The dog made a bow;
The dame said "Your servant",
The dog said "Bow-wow".

Even famous poets whose books are set for examinations enjoyed a bit of a joke – like John Keats. As well as his odes "On A Grecian Urn" and "To a Nightingale", he also wrote this rhyme –

There Was a Naughty Boy

There was a naughty boy,
A naughty boy was he,
He would not stop at home,
He could not quiet be
He took
In his knapsack
A book
Full of vowels
And a shirt
With some towels,
A slight cap
For night cap,
A hair brush,
Comb ditto,
New stockings –
For old ones
Would split O!
This knapsack
Tight at's back
He rivetted close
And followed his nose
To the North
To the North,
And followed his nose
To the North.

Strangely enough you can find some of the funniest poems in churchyards, written on tombstones.

On Mary Ann Lowder

Here lies the body of Mary Ann Lowder
She burst while drinking a seidlitz powder.
Called from this world to her heavenly rest,
She should have waited till it effervesced.

You can find another one in Winchester Churchyard, on
the tomb of Thomas Thetcher, a Grenadier in the North
Regiment of the Hampshire Militia, who died on 12 May
1764.

Here sleeps in peace a Hampshire Grenadier,
Who caught his death by drinking cold small beer,
Soldiers, be wise from his untimely fall,
And when you're hot, drink strong, or
None at all.

After a while, the idea caught on, and people made up
tombstone rhymes just for the fun of it. This one's called
"*Willie's Epitaph*", but nobody knows who wrote it.

Little Willie from his mirror
Licked the mercury right off,
Thinking, in his childish error,
It would cure the whooping cough.
At the funeral his mother
Smartly said to Mrs Brown:
" 'Twas a chilly day for Willie
When the mercury went down."

Edward Lear is probably best known for his limericks, but
he wrote a great deal of other comic verse. Here's part of his
poem about a very curious creature.

The Quangle-Wangle's Hat

On the top of the Crumpetty Tree
   The Quangle-Wangle sat.
But his face you could not see
   On account of his Beaver Hat.
For his Hat was a hundred and two feet wide,
With ribbons and bibbons on every side
And bells, and buttons, and loops, and lace,
So that nobody ever could see the face
   Of the Quangle-Wangle Quee.

The Quangle-Wangle said
   To himself on the Crumpetty Tree:
"Jam; and jelly; and bread;
   Are the best of food for me!
But the longer I live on this Crumpetty Tree,
The plainer than ever it seems to me
That very few people come this way,
And that life on the whole is far from gay!"
   Said the Quangle-Wangle Quee.

Another great writer, well known for tales like *Alice's Adventures in Wonderland* and *Through the Looking Glass*, also enjoyed making up funny poems. He was Lewis Carroll, a mathematician and a clergyman, but that didn't stop him having a terrific sense of humour.

The Mad Gardener's Song

He thought he saw an Elephant,
That practised on a fife:
He looked again, and found it was
A letter from his wife.
"At length I realise," he said,
"The bitterness of Life!"

He thought he saw a Buffalo
Upon the chimney-piece:
He looked again, and found it was
His Sister's Husband's Niece.
"Unless you leave this house," he said,
"I'll send for the Police!"

He thought he saw a Rattlesnake
That questioned him in Greek:
He looked again, and found it was
The Middle of Next Week.
"The one thing I regret," he said,
"Is that it cannot speak!"

He thought he saw a Banker's Clerk
Descending from the bus:
He looked again, and found it was
A Hippopotamus:
"If this should stay to dine," he said,
"There won't be much for us!"

He thought he saw a Kangaroo
That worked a coffee-mill:
He looked again, and found it was
A Vegetable-Pill.
"Were I to swallow this," he said,
"I should be very ill!"

He thought he saw a Coach-and-Four
That stood beside his bed:
He looked again, and found it was
A Bear without a Head.
"Poor thing," he said, "poor silly thing!
It's waiting to be fed!"

He thought he saw an Albatross
That fluttered round the lamp:
He looked again, and found it was
A Penny-Postage-Stamp.

"You'd best be getting home," he said:
"The nights are very damp!"

He thought he saw a Garden-Door
That opened with a key:
He looked again, and found it was
A double Rule of Three:
"And all its mystery," he said,
"Is clear as day to me!"

He thought he saw an Argument
That proved he was the Pope:
He looked again, and found it was
A Bar of Mottled Soap.
"A fact so dread," he faintly said,
"Extinguishes all hope!"

Not all funny poems are as well known as that. We'd never come cross Edward Abbott Parry before, and considering he was born in 1863, his "Jam Fish" poem sounds extremely modern!

The Jam Fish

A Jam Fish sat on his hard-bake rock,
His head in his left hand fin,
He was knitting his wife a sky-blue sock,
With second-hand rolling pin.

His wife was watching her old Aunt Brill
Sew acid drops on his shirt,
While his grandmother fitted a caramel frill
To a Butterscotch tartan skirt.

His cousin Jelly Fish swam
In a pool of parsley sauce,
While the Jam Fish sighed, "I am only Jam,
And must wait for the second course.
When rice mould quivers on the dish
And shakes at the children's sneers,
Till the scented voice of the old Jam Fish
Shall melt their scorn to tears."

The American Ogden Nash wrote some of the best-known comic verses of *this* century. Most of them were first published in magazines, and everyone enjoyed them so much, they got printed again and again. You can find them in all sorts of books of collected verse. Ogden Nash's poems are often short, sharp and to the point!

The Canary

The Song of Canaries
Never varies
And when they're moulting
They're pretty revolting.

The Termite

Some primal termite knocked on wood
And tasted it, and found it good,
And that is why your Cousin May
Fell through the parlour floor to-day.

Reflection on Babies

A bit of talcum
Is always walcum

In the 1950s the most hilarious programme on the radio was the Goon Show, and one of the Goons, Spike Milligan, is also a poet. Like Edward Lear and Lewis Carroll, he enjoys writing nonsense like this poem:

On The Ning Nang Nong

On the Ning Nang Nong
Where the Cows go Bong!
And the Monkeys all say Boo!
There's a Nong Nang Ning
Where the trees go Ping!
And the tea pots Jibber Jabber Joo.
On the Nong Ning Nang
All the mice go Clang!
And you just can't catch 'em when they do!
So it's Ning Nang Nong!
Cows go Bong!
Nong Nang Ning!
Trees go Ping!
Nong Ning Nang!
The mice go Clang!
What a noisy place to belong,
Is the Ning Nang Ning Nang Nong!!

Spike also wrote about animals in the zoo – but it's not exactly a nature poem, it's called:

Look at All Those Monkeys

Look at all those monkeys
Jumping in their cage.
Why don't they all go out to work
And earn a decent wage?

How can you say such silly things,
And you a son of mine?
Imagine monkeys travelling on
The Morden – Edgware line!

But what about the Pekinese!
They have an allocation.
"Don't travel during Peke hour",
It says on every station.

My Gosh, you're right, my clever boy,
I never thought of that!
And so they left the monkey house,
While an elephant raised his hat.

But of all comic verse, so far as we know, Odd Odes are the only ones that have these rules:

First of all, think of a funny name – like Jeremiah Jerk or Bertha Boot. Make the lines rhyme in pairs with a rhyme like this:

Ti tum ti tum ti tum ti tum
Ti tum ti tum ti tum ti tum

If you carry on like that you're bound to end up with an Odd Ode. Cyril Fletcher, the Inventor of the Odd Ode, says thirty lines is about the best length, and subject and content of the ode must be "extravagantly fanciful".

Although Cyril Fletcher first broadcast his Odd Odes in 1936 and had actually written his very first ones at school, it was in the 1940s they became really famous. With air raids and bombs falling the people of Britain did not go out at night – they stayed indoors and listened to their radios instead, and Cyril's Odes were a real tonic. They made people forget their worries about the war and gave them a badly needed laugh.

The Odd Odes are always about people getting into extraordinary situations, and Cyril recites them putting on all sorts of different voices for the characters.

Matilda Morgan

This tells of poor Matilda Morgan,
Who had an outsize nasal organ,
From whence like some loud-speaker roared,
Most fearful noises when she snored;
These rose in quite a scale ascending,
Until a violent snort came rending,
Then with gurgle as of pain,
Would start the same tune round again.
The sleepless neighbours used to stir,
And murmur "Lumee! hark at her!"
While some, with manners prim, got shirty
Who thought the noises sounded dirty.
Her brother then, facetious pup,
Said "Can't you bung that hooter up?"
And suiting action to his talk,
He plugged each nostril with a cork,
But found with each succeeding snort,
They popped out with a loud report,
And just like bullets from a gun,
Shot all her toes off, one by one.
Then poor Matilda, feeling weak,
Applied a clothes-peg to her beak,
But found the snort confirmed her fears,
And simply backfired through her ears,
Which made them flap so much about
The draught blew all her curlers out,
So now she's gone, though sad at heart,
And in a lighthouse plays her part,
For when there's fog impeding craft,
Matilda takes a sleeping draught,
And sailors hearing snore and snort,
Can guide their vessels into port.

Willie Plank

This is the tale of Willie Plank,
Who learned to drive an Army tank,
And, feeling very pleased with life,
He drove it home to show his wife.
And said "Old Fannie won't half laugh
To see me coming up the parf."
Alas, for Willie's bright idea,
For, as he changed to second gear,
He gasped "Coo, strewf – I won't half cop it,
I never asked 'em how to stop it!"
He crashed his way through garden wall
Across the lawn and through the hall,
And mounting to the second floor,
Went rumbling through the bathroom door,
Behind of which his better half
Was sitting knees-up in the barf.
Poor Fannie Plank, annoyed and shocked,
Said "Blimey, and it never knocked."
Then covered up her girlish blushes
With loofah, towel and scrubbing brushes.
Meanwhile the tank, to its disgrace,
Heaved bath and inmate into space,
And rumbled down the stairs non-stop
With Fannie Plank perched high on top,
Trying to don a bathroom rug
With one foot caught up in the plug,
A dab of soap upon her snout,
And draughts all up the plughole spout!
They rattled slowly down the hill,
Where people gazed, as people will,
And yelled – "Coo look" and some said "Cor!
It's weapons week to help the war."
So quickly passing round the cap,
They tossed their coins in Fannie's lap.

At length the tank came to a stop
And Fannie clambered off the top
In bath-rug, towel and loofah dressed
And five-and-fourpence on her chest.

When Cyril came to Blue Peter he wrote Odd Odes all about
the three of us – we thought they were excellent!

John's Ode

This is the tale of Johnny Noakes
The keenest of all climbing blokes.
He climbed the H M S Ganges' mast,
And Battersea Power Station chimney fast.
He's also climbed up a trapeze
And Crystal Palace Aerial if you please.
And soiling his new suit of nylon
He climbed up an electric pylon,
A thing no one should ever do –
In case you get a shock or two.
John did – then saw some nasty flashes,
We thought that he'd return as ashes.
He's just the same now I suppose
But he can plug an electric toaster in his nose,
And the kitchen mixer for his cooking
He will plug in his ear when no one's looking.
You may think this is a trifle cruel
But it don't 'alf save the nation's fuel!

Peter's Ode

The thing that Peter Purves likes
Is riding about on motor bikes.
One day for a Blue Peter stunt,
He put his coat on back to front.

Then he fell off and came a cropper,
And was discovered by a lady copper.
And thinking he was front to back,
She twisted him around, alack.
Seizing his knapper in a bound,
She gave it a wrench and turned it round.
Coming to, poor Peter rose,
And with his hand, sought his nose,
But groping round, he found instead,
Another portion of his head.
To this police-woman now he's wed,
He married the girl who turned his head.

Lesley's Ode

Lesley Judd got awfully cross,
Her horse would play at pitch and toss,
And every fence when told to jump,
Would land her sadly on her rump,
So on her horse she sat a-straddle,
And glued her breeches to the saddle.
Then hurling o'er a clump of gorse,
She jumped much higher than the horse.
There was a sound of rending stitches,
That played awful havoc with her breeches,
And although her pride was very hurt,
She walked off wearing a grass skirt!

These special Blue Peter Odd Odes got our Competition off to a very good start. Sparked off by Cyril's ideas, thousands of Odd Odes came pouring in and in this book you can read the Top Prize Winning Odes, and some of the best of the Runners-Up.

We hope you enjoy reading them as much as we did.

And remember, the next time it's a rainy day or you're ill in bed, or on a long train journey try your hand at an Odd Ode. It's not all that difficult, and your family and friends will enjoy hearing them!

John Dookes

Peter Purves   *Lesley Judd.*

Prizewinners

A lady by the name of Clare
Found a bird's nest in her hair,
She tried to move it with a brush
And from her hair there flew a thrush.
She said: "Good gracious, stone the crows!"
And then an egg splashed on her nose.
So now she always takes good care
To wear a hair net on her hair.

David Roberts
Age: 7

This is the tale of Bertha Brown,
Who had the biggest nose in town.

One day while at her place of learning
She said, "Please Miss, there's something burning."

"You'd better tell old Farmer Brown
That his haystack's burning down."

And sure enough two miles away,
They found a pile of smouldering hay.

Now Bertha's got her just rewards,
Her likeness will be in Tussaud's.

The only reason for delay,
Her nose requires extra clay.

Andrew Ridley
Age: 7

My mother's name is Mary Fox,
She has some stripey football socks,
A Christmas present from my dad,
She really thought he was quite mad.
At night she wears them when in bed,
To keep her feet from going red
With cold. You see she soon feels ill
Without her socks she gets a chill.
One day she saw a football game,
She wore her socks to spread her fame.
And then approached the manager's gate
She knocked and said, "Am I too late?"
"You are," replied the manager's wife,
"He's gone on holiday up to Fife."
"I must play football," said my Mum,
The lady then looked rather glum.
"Well if you wish you'd better hasten
Up to Fife to ask permission."
Without a pause to change her dress
She flew to Fife and he said "yes".
She got many goals for her home team
So she became extremely keen.
But now she's given the whole thing up
She did not win a single cup.

Deborah Fox
Age: 7

First Prize

A young girl by the name of Nelly,
Was told to make a king-size jelly.
It was to be a star attraction,
And Nelly was a girl of action.

When told there need not be a limit,
She used 500 packets in it.
Raspberry, orange, lemon, lime,
She really had a busy time.

To solve her first and foremost wish,
She'd have to find a monstrous dish.
After a long and studied think,
She thought she'd make it in the sink.

The sink turned out to be too small,
So Nelly thought she'd have a ball.
It really would be quite a laugh,
To make a jelly in the bath.

Soon her dad, a tired bloke,
Thought he'd have a quiet soak.
But he didn't like the notion,
Of his daughter's setting lotion.

> Robert Marsh
> Age: 10

This is the tale of Betty Box,
Who loved to stuff herself with chocs.
She ate them all day long at school,
Although it was against the rule.
Each day when she got home to Mum,
Her mother said: "Your poor old tum –
It must be empty, come and eat,"
And piled her plate with veg and meat.
Poor Betty, full of chocs you see,
Couldn't eat a single pea.
"I just can't eat it Mum," she said,
"I think perhaps I'll go to bed."
This went on for quite some time,
Till Mrs Box one day said, "I'm –
Beginning to wonder what's the matter,
Our Betty's getting fatter and fatter."
She said to Bet, "You should be thinner,
You never seem to eat your dinner!"
Then one day stuffed with milk and plain,
Poor Betty got an awful pain.
Her big fat tum was overloaded,
And with a BANG! she just exploded.
So if you're fond of sweets and chocs,
Just remember Betty Box.

Anne Hunt
Age: 10

This is the story of Jonathan Wails
Who used to keep pet slimy snails.
One day one crawled up mother's leg
Who screamed and squashed it with a peg.
Poor Jonathan was very sad
To think his little snail was dead.
All the snails they crowded round
To see their brother on the ground.
One small snail called Timothy Tenge
Decided he would take revenge,
And with the other snails he led
Them to the wicked mother's bed.
They started up the leg and down
The bumpy, lumpy eiderdown.
As mother was just going to sleep,
Around her body they did creep.
One sat upon her crooked nose
Another crawled upon her toes.
And when this mother did awake,
Their trails wound round her like a snake,
She stared and jumped right out of bed,
And on the ceiling hit her head.
She packed her case and left that day,
And where she's gone I cannot say.
The moral of this story's clear,
Do not believe all that you hear.

Sandra Bundy
Age: 9

This is the tale of Nellie Smails,
Who decided not to cut her nails,
She said, "I get in such contortions,
Trying to reach my lower portions."
Every time that she went shopping
Through her shoes her nails kept popping,
A crowd would gather in the street
To stare at Nellie's spiky feet.
One lad shouted: "Come and see
This one should be up a tree."
But went off howling very quick
When Nellie placed a well-aimed kick.
One day into a park she wandered
And by the duck pond sat and pondered.
The keeper said, "Well what do you know
How did you get them things to grow?"
"Here Sam," he murmured with a titter,
"She can help us clear our litter."
So she is famous is our Nellie,
You've probably seen her on the telly.
But if into that park you stray,
Don't forget to watch the way,
Nellie Smails with gestures neat
Collects the litter with her feet.

Alison West
Age: 12

Collects the litter with her feet

This is the tale of Lucy Grant,
Who bought a little indoor plant.
She put it in a small green pot,
And placed it by her brother's cot.
But when the night was passed and gone,
So had Lucy's brother, John.
Then Lucy noticed, with surprise,
The plant had grown to twice its size.
She looked again and found it had
Put tendrils round her Mum and Dad!
Her Mum and Dad were pulled inside,
The plant's mouth, that was open wide!
Lucy, soon, had trained her plant,
To eat, on sight, a Gran or Aunt.
In a week, the plant ate whole
Six cats, three dogs, a mouse and mole.
The plant devoured both man and beast
And added Lucy to its fcast.
So ends this tale of Lucy Grant,
Who met her end, clutched by her plant.

Steven Weller
Age: 13

Little Willy full of glee,
Found a flea upon a tree.
He put the flea upon his head,
And took it home to find a bed.
As he was walking through the woods,
He found six hundred Christmas puds.
"They're just the things," he shouted out,
"To make my flea both big and stout.
I aim to have the biggest flea,
That anyone could ever see.
With these puds so fat and round,
My flea will be the fattest found."
The flea began to eat and eat
And very soon it had big feet.
The flea began to swell and grow,
And soon was ready for a show.
The great day dawned, both clear and bright,
The flea had reached enormous height.
It was eight feet above the ground
And measured ninety inches round.
They set off to the show with joy,
That mighty flea and puny boy.
The sight of these two in the town,
Caused folks to pull their shutters down.
They cowered in corners, under beds,
They shrieked and howled and hid their heads.
This wailing noise disturbed the flea,
"I'm mighty hungry now," said he.
"There's only bread to eat out here,"
Said Willy turning pale with fear.
"Bread," said the flea, "I want my pud!"

Said Willy, "It is in the wood."
And then came Willy's fatal error,
Instead of running home in terror,
He stood his ground, and so you see,
Was gobbled by the flea for tea!

Mark Priestley
Age: 11

Runners-Up

There was a sleepy man called Fred,
Who would not get up from his bed.
He stayed in bed the live-long day
Because he loved to stay that way.
One day his mother said, "Now Fred,
You must get up and leave your bed,
Go on – get up upon your feet,
Because I must wash your dirty sheet."
He moved but fell upon his beak,
Because his legs were very weak.
The pain did turn his eyes to water,
To exercise he really did oughter,
So then he tried to touch his toes,
But caught his arm up in his clothes.
He rolled and rolled across the floor,
And out and through the bedroom door,
Across the landing, down the stair.
(He had fainted so he didn't care!)
He ended up in a hospital bed,
"I never should have got up," he said!

Duncan Palmer
Age: 6

I know a man called Peter Farr,
Who owns a most remarkable car.
I know you will think it rather bonkers
But instead of petrol he uses conkers.
And if you hear the engine wheeze
That is because it's made of cheese.
And when you sit upon the seat
You will find it is made of sausage meat!
The radiator is filled with flour,
Which gives the car a lot of power,
The tyres of the car sometimes squeal,
Because each is made of a conger eel,
And if the car comes to a halt,
You will find you've given it too much salt!

     Christopher Hardy
     Age: 7

This is the tale of Jumbo Pears,
Who had the most enormous ears,
So big, that on a windy day
He flapped them and he flew away.
He flew to France and then to Spain
And then he flew back home again.
Now he flies there twice a day.
With people on his back each way.
Now if you haven't seen him yet.
He calls himself a Jumbo Jet.

Jonathan Miles
Age: 7

This is the tale of Erica's Mummy,
Who stuck a pin into her tummy,
Then not knowing what to do,
She took an aspirin or two,
And then she thought she'd go to bed,
But she fell down and bumped her head.
"Oh, what shall I do now?" said she,
And then sat down and had her tea.
But still she had not moved the pin,
When she sat down it stuck right in!
"Oh! Oh!" she shouted out in pain,
"I'll have to go to bed again."
Then Daddy called the doctor in.
And said, "Please will you move this pin."
The doctor did it straight away.
Then Mummy was all bright and gay.

Erica Kemhadjian
Age: 7

There was a man who came from space
Who had a long thin orange face,
He came to earth and landed hard,
Right in the middle of my back yard,
He got out of his rocket ship
And felt his trousers start to rip,
He said, "I'm cold at my rear end,
Have you some trousers you could lend?"
I told him mine would be too small
But I'd ask my bigger brother Paul,
He came into my house to wait
And said "hello" to my mummy Kate.
He donned the trousers that I had lent
Said "Thank you," and off he went.
His ship took off on route to Mars.
Paul's trousers for ever among the stars.

    Caron Morgan
    Age: 7

And felt his trousers start to rip

There was a boy called Johnny Spears
Who had the most enormous ears.
And every time the wind would blow
Up into the cloudy sky he'd go.
One day when playing on the beach,
He suddenly rose far out of reach
Of his Mamma, sunbathing there,
And floated off into the air.

A passing gull with startled cry
Watched, as young John went flying by.
A sailing yacht far, far down there,
Whose captain could only stand and stare,
Promptly hit a rock and sank,
While crowds collected on the bank.
His mother watched in great dismay
As John went flying far away.
The English Channel soon he crossed,
By every playful wind being tossed,
The Eiffel Tower caused some dismay,
In tearing half his pants away,
And when he left warm Italy's shore,
The Leaning Tower leaned ever more!
He was last seen by a passing whale
Blown out of course by a summer gale,
With flapping ears and open mouth
Heading towards the icy south.
The lesson of this ode should be,
Before you go down to the sea
If extra large, pin back your ears
And don't be like poor Johnny Spears.

Muriel Johnson
Age: 10

I tell the tale of Nellie Grise,
Who did insist on crossing eyes,
Her mother said, "You silly girl,
You'll get yourself in an awful twirl.
The wind will change and they'll be stuck,
And what a silly girl you'll look!"
Nellie, no notice of her took –
Eyes crossed – wind changed – what awful luck!
Nellie found to her dismay,
That cross-eyed look was here to stay,
And now she finds when she sheds tears,
They miss her face and soak her ears.

Lynne Taft
Age: 10

This is an ode to my form teacher,
When he shouts he ain't 'alf a screecher.
He raps his pen upon the table,
The ink spurts out on my friend Mabel.
When in class I eat my lunch,
He says, "Who's making that rude crunch?"
In fright I drop it on the floor,
Just as the head comes through the door
Upon my milky bar he slides,
Doing a quick-step and a glide,
As he rises to his feet,
He slips again upon his seat!
With a ranting and a roar
He slides with ease right through the door,
Down the corridor careering –
To the whistling and the cheering –
Round and round like a spinning top –
He becomes entangled with a mop!
Quick as a flash he grabs the handle,
Shouting, "Oh I feel like a Roman candle."
With fury he backs through the door,
Clutching his rear and shouting, "No more."

Melanie Wood
Age: 10

There was a girl named Sally Skinner,
Who always ate sardines for dinner.
One day she ate the tin as well
And so her tum began to swell.
Her mother said, "My dear, good grief!"
"Gosh, golly!" said her brother Keef.
At last her tummy stopped quite still,
But poor Sally Skinner felt so ill.
She had some nasty stuff to take,
Which seemed to cure her tummy ache.
Her mother bought her buns to eat
Sally knew they were a treat.
Alas! She was so stuffed with tin.
She had to chuck them in the bin.
Poor Sally could not touch her dinner,
And so she slowly grew much thinner.
One night she sadly walked to bed
Next morning her brother found her dead.
So that was the end of Sally Skinner
And now she never has sardines for dinner!

Lydia Callaway
Age: 8

This is the tale of Eric Spratt,
Who had a most peculiar cat.
His eyes were mauve, his ears were red
His green hair piled up on his head!
Poor Eric led a lonely life,
For all he wanted was a wife,
The thing that put them off was that,
They'd have to live with that darn cat!
And so he advertised to find
A woman who was colour blind!
He found a girl to fit the bill,
But all her clothes made him feel ill:
Her hat was blue – her scarf was green –
The biggest mess he'd ever seen!
And so he decided that
He'd better stick to his old cat!

Julian Blake
Age: 9

47

I had a dog whose name was Rose,
Who loved to lick all human toes,
At the sight of naked feet
Her canine heart increased its beat.
"Ha, ha," she'd bark with quite a giggle,
"I'll soon make those ten digits wriggle."
"Oh, dear," I thought with some alarm,
"One day that dog will do some harm."
To her I said in tones severe
That tongue to toe should ne'er come near.
All went well, till one fine day,
Auntie Maggie came to stay,
And taking hard the summer's heat,
Decided she would bathe her feet.
So sitting on a milking stool,
She dipped them in the swimming pool!
Rosie took a flying leap,
Knocked Auntie Maggie in a heap,
And though she knew she didn't oughta
Pushed poor old Auntie in the water!
Now I'm afraid it's R.I.P.
Neither dog, nor aunt, could swim you see.

Shona Saul
Age: 10

Pushed poor old Auntie in the water!

This is the tale of wee Billy McCorran,
Who tripped and fell right over his sporran,
As he went down with a crash and a plonk
He yelled, "Ouch, I think I've broken me conk."
His big brother said, "Quick, hop onto my scooter,
And we'll go get the doc to fix up your hooter."
But Billy, dripping with blood and tears,
Said of the old doc, "I have some fears
His only cure for the nasal disaster
Will be to patch it up with sticking plaster."
Now Billy's Mum when she saw her young son,
Said, "Oh my wee Laddie what have you done?"
And with a rolling of sleeves and nary a hitch,
She started to doctor up her poor Billy's snitch.
Young Billy, who was sniffling and moaning with pain
Declared: "I won't be wearing the kilt again.
A pair of trousers I will don
To cover up my sit upon."
For though Billy's a Scot, and this is the point,
'Twas the kilt that put his nose out of joint
And the moral is plain for all kilties to see
Don't wear your sporran below the knee
For like Billy you may trip and fall
And end up in the hos-pit-all.

Hendry McIntosh
Age: 9

This is the tale of Liza Green
Who hoped to be sweet-making queen,
Said she, when lessons were complete,
"I must try cooking with my feet!"
So she turned her feet to making toffee,
And flavoured it with mild blend coffee,
While stirring, some slopped on the floor,
And Liza found she could move no more!
Stuck to the floor, her hands so bare,
Her two legs waving in the air.
"Oh dear," she cried, "oh, help me please,
The toffee's dripping on my knees!"
Her neighbours tried with might and main.
To get poor Liza free again.
Her cries rang out, "What shall I do?"
But the coffee toffee had set like glue.
Her neighbours came with butter, lard,
Soap and water, and tried hard.
To prise poor Liza from the floor,
And stand her on her feet once more.
Alas, alack she had to stay,
And for all I know is there today.
Warning all, when making sweets
Use your hands and not your feets!

> Jonathan Ryder
> Age: 10

There was a girl called Graceful Grace,
Who had a very charming face,
And would have been quite free of hate,
Had it not been for her great weight.
She gained a pound in every week,
And people were quite scared and meek
When they heard our Grace a-coming,
Her feet upon the pavement drumming.
But she made a lot of trouble,
Reducing everything to rubble,
Every time that she passed through,
'Twas this that made her feel quite blue.
So her parents did agree,
"To the country, move will we."
Out of the town Grace was content,
But ruined the environment!
Because of Grace's heavy weight,
(She now weighed twenty stone and eight)
Mother suggested a dancing school,
Father said she was a fool!
But mother made her "little" Grace
A pretty "little" dress of lace,
And sent her to the dancing school,
Grace protested she was cruel!
Mother sent her all the same –
In two hours back again she came.
"The ballet mistress was upset,
The roof fell in on my pirouette."
"Oh dear, oh dear," her mother cried,
"Did you spread the wreckage wide?
Will they be sending us the bill?"

The roof fell in on my pirouette

"Yes," said Grace, and felt quite ill.
Now brother Bert came to the fore –
(His line was selling good hard-core).
He told them of his bright idea.
"Yes," his father cried, "here, here!"
Grace is now employed by Bert,
And she would be so very hurt,
If you tried to intervene,
With her job as a crushing machine!

      Elisabeth Millington
      Age: 10

Here is a tale of Mabel Quirk,
Who rode a cycle to her work,
And one day when the road was wet,
Poor Mabel, flying like a jet
Sailed through the air, and so did fall,
At the feet of a policeman tall.
"What goes on 'ere?" the bobbie said,
Surveying Mabel, blushing red.
"You can't park 'ere, the notice says."
He stooped and tried the girl to raise.
Then Mabel's heart began to thump,
Her feet were tangled in the pump,
And tears within her throat did choke,
Poor girl had sat upon a spoke!
So Mabel with complex inferior
Took home the spoke in her posterior!

    Heather Rogerson
    Age: 10

Every night young Mervin Hoots,
Went to bed wearing wellington boots,
His wife, Matilda, quite upset,
Said, "Aren't your feet rather wet?"
Yawning loudly, Mervin rose,
Producing welly-covered toes.
Matilda cried, "I've had enough"
And then began to get quite rough,
Lamps and vases flew so fast,
Mervin thought he'd breathed his last,
At last he crept from under cover,
And cried, "I'm going home to mother!"
So Mervin Hoots ran for his life,
She even chased him up to Fife,
He found a boat and took a chance,
And ended up in southern France,
Through Spain and Greece and then Japan,
Through India and Afghanistan,
Then further north he made his way,
Until he found a place to stay,
So now with wellies lined with fur,
Mervin sleeps and does not stir,
For there amid the ice and snow,
He's living with an Eskimo!

Patrick Shepherd
Age: 10

There amid the ice and snow,
He's living with an Eskimo!

Gymnastics Jane they always said,
Loved standing up upon her head,
Her mother cried: "Now don't do that,"
As Jane fell down upon the cat.
One day while in a backward bend,
She slipped her arm around her friend,
Both locked in this position fast,
The Fire Brigade were called at last.
"Never seen such a queer sight,
Two girls stuck together tight!
We'll try to help in any way,
But in this plight you'll have to stay."
When next you're shopping in the street
Don't be surprised if Jane you meet
Locked together with her friend
Rolling around in a backward bend.

Elaine Forbes
Age: 10

This is the tale of Lizzie Pike
Who once got caught on a nasty spike.
"Ough," she cried, "whatever next!
Good gracious me! I do feel vexed.
I only went out for a walk
Not to be caught on a rusty stalk."
And as eyes travelled to and from,
"I'm all right there, it's my poor bum."
And as folk talked one to the other,
Liz yelled, "Will someone fetch my mother!"
Mum came fast, applied some butter,
And soon Liz shot into the gutter,
Slithering there all wet and drippy,
She cried, "Ooh Mum! My bum's all slippy!"
Mum said, "Lizzie, with that there seater,
I think you should be on Blue Peter."

Anthony Murphy
Age: 10

There was a girl called Ethel White,
Who had a frightful appetite.
She swallowed everything she could,
From bits of string to planks of wood!
One day she ate a great big plum,
Which began to grow inside her tum.
Her mother said, "Oh dear! Oh dear!
There's something coming from your ear,
It looks rather like a twig,
Go and wash, you dirty pig!"
Soon branches sprouted from her head,
Her father went into the shed.
He came back with the garden shears
And started clipping round her ears.
Suddenly they heard her squeak,
They looked inside and saw a beak.
"It's a bird!" they cried. "It's made a nest!
It's got some babies, well I'm blessed!"
Her sister said, "You useful thing,
I'll use you for my garden swing."
When Christmas came she looked a treat,
With silver bells around her feet,
And tinsel hanging from her head,
And Christmas lights in blue and red.

Hilary Trollope
Age: 9

And started clipping round her ears

Lady Annabella West,
Began to knit herself a vest,
She knitted fast, she knitted long;
She knitted all her stitches wrong.
The vest it trailed along the floor,
Down the step and out the door,
Along the Great North Road it ran,
And caused a fearful traffic jam!
It covered mountains, hills, and ditches,
And had the people all in stitches.
As fear and chaos filled the world
Lady A. just plain and purled.
The police put posters all in red,
WANTED VEST, ALIVE OR DEAD!
At last the vest had reached the sea,
And Lady A. had stopped for tea,
As Annabella munched and ground,
The vest just slowly sank, and DROWNED!

> Louise Hampton
> Age: 9

Here is the tale of Tortoise Fred,
Who wouldn't eat what he was fed.
He got so thin, his cough was chronic.
The Doctor said: "Give him a tonic!"
This really knocked him off his feet,
He had to take it with a sweet.
And then one day while off his legs,
He went and laid a dozen eggs.
This caused the BBC to worry,
Put Biddy Baxter in a flurry.
A meeting of Blue Peter staff,
Where all were trying not to laff,
Decided that, to save their face,
Another pet should take his place.
A PIG? A SNAKE? A PINK CANARY?
Or for John a Spider Hairy?
Then a happy thought came to their leader,
From now on Fred will be our Freda!

Sally Barnes
Age: 8

This is the tale of dear old Bill,
Who munched straight through a window sill!
When he'd finished the greenhouse door,
He started on our bedroom floor!
And to his family's giggling laughter,
He gobbled up a great big rafter!
Then when asked if that was all
Said, "No," and ate our garden wall!
The next day all was quiet,
The doctor said, "You must diet."
From that day on Bill ate matchsticks,
And now he's eating low calorie plastics.

Pamela Brown
Age: 10

This is the tale of Sally Nashon,
Who, for eating, had a passion.
She started on a candlestick,
Ate everything from wax to wick.
Not satisfied with this, she ate
Her way through one bone-china plate;
(This did not please her mum at all)
And then her eye met something small,
Small but lethal, as we shall see,
But Sally gulped it down with glee –
A set of chessmen, all complete
For Sal 'twas but a bit to eat.
Her ravenous hunger searched again
And led her to the window-pane,
Where the poor girl found great pleasure,
In picking the paint off, at her leisure;
She chewed it up and spat it out –
She was insane! There was no doubt.
In the morning, Sal did wake
With a tremendous tummy-ache
No longer, for eating, had she a passion
For days her food was on short ration.
She'd eaten to such a huge degree
Poor Sal now lies in a cemetery.

Kay Ford
Age: 12

This is an ode to Mary-Ann
Who was an ardent pop-group fan.
Her bedroom walls were all adorned
With pictures that her mother scorned.
At all the concerts she would shriek,
Until so hoarse she could not speak.
Her dad said, "Mary's round the bend
With all this mad pop-music trend."
But on his words she did not brood
And remained in her ecstatic mood.
To work she would not give a thought,
Although her parents knew she ought.
She did not want to go to school
Because she didn't like the rule
That radios could not be played,
(The Head didn't like the noise they made).
Mum knew that she would do no good
If she neglected work and food,
For she had eaten nothing more
Than three baked beans and eggs, all raw
(Her idol was on hunger strike,
Against all things he didn't like).
Of her fast she did not tire,
And soon her limbs were thin as wire.
Her parents had a terrible fear
That she would soon all disappear.
She listened all the day to discs,
Not knowing she took so many risks.
One night the wind was blowing strong,
And although she knew that she was wrong,
She opened wide the window pane,

In rushed the wind, in came the rain!
It whisked the girl right off her feet,
And swept her down into the street,
Her weakened form just could not fight,
And off she went into the night,
Until she reached a leafy lane,
Where she trickled slowly down a drain!
Although this tale is quite fantastic,
It's good advice to a pop fanatic.
Pop idols are all very well,
It may be nice to scream and yell
But when thinking of their groovy sound,
Keep your feet firm on the ground!

      Mary Moore
      Age: 14

This is the tale of a poor hippy named Joe,
For whatever he tried his beard wouldn't grow,
He'd look in the mirror and he'd rant and he'd rave,
"Oh, why won't it grow though I never shave."
His hair it was red and curly and long,
And with his moustache he could find nothing wrong.
His sideboards were long and as bushy could be,
But on his poor chin not a hair could he see.
Dressed in his hippy gear he looked quite a lad,
But without a hairy chin no girl would share his pad.
Every hair restorer on the market he did try,
But each was a failure – how he did sigh!
At last he bought a false beard and stuck it on with glue,
Now Joe was very happy and his dream came true,
The first time he wore it to go out with his mate –
Oh, dear me, what a tragedy so sadly we relate,
He struck a match and held it just to light a fag
And his beard went up in flames like an oily rag
At this Joe cried, "Oh crikey, my hopes at last have sank,
I'm off to get my hair cut and go work in the bank."

David Smith
Age: 13

There was a girl called Mary Rose,
Who had a lumpy turned-up nose,
Her friends all teased her of her "whiffer,"
Said she, "It is a smashing sniffer!"
When passing by a sweety shop,
With one big snort she got the lot,
Chocolate drops and jelly jubes,
All went the same way down her tubes.
Her mum took her to Doctor Dose
Who thought about her awful nose,
Said he, "I've seen some wondrous snorters,
But never one quite like your daughter's."
One day when visiting a grocery store
She solved her problem for evermore,
She caught her nose in a bacon slicer,
All agreed it looked much nicer.

    Susan Bridge
    Age: 11

This is the tale of Harry Best,
Who wore an army surplus vest.
He said to all, "Without a doubt,
This vest's the best that is about."
And trying to prove that he was right,
He wore the thing both day and night,
One night, whilst lying in his room,
And unaware of pending doom
He was dreaming he was Jimmy Saville,
When the army vest chose to unravel
Since army vests are made of string,

He soon got tangled in the thing
And before he'd muttered, "What the heck!"
The vest was wound around his neck.
So now to end this tale of woe
For poor old Harry had to go.
So let him not have died in vain
Remember, it is to your gain
Should anyone offer you a vest
To think of Harry, who's at rest
With on his gravestone, plain to see,
"I wore a vest, and it killed me."

     Sandra Williams
     Age: 14

This is the sad tale of Mrs Rangle,
Who got her nose caught in a mangle.
And when at last she pulled it out,
It looked just like a water spout.
"Goodness," her friends all said, "what a hooter!
We shouldn't say it, but it don't 'alf suit her."
Around the world the poor soul went
To find her nose some special treatment.
But now she laughs at friends who hurt her,
Because she met the brothers McWhirter
Who measured her conk with two long cords
And entered it in their Book of Records.

Sean Allen
Age: 11

This is the tale of Nelly Bracket
Who bought herself a tennis racket.
Her husband Fred was quite dismayed
At this energetic game she played.
Be it sun or be it rain
Nelly had tennis on the brain,
Fred built a court upon the lawn
Perhaps it was no Wimbledon,
But Nelly rubbed her hands with glee
And cried, "This is the game for me."
Her friends all hid behind the hut,
Whenever they heard balls hit gut.
And with one voice they all would cry,
"Now don't you hit them balls too high."
But Nelly yelled, "I'm the best yet,"
And balls went flying like a jet.
Then at last her great day came
When she was asked to have a game
Against the world's number one,
And so the battle it begun
Nelly led right to the end,
Her country's honour to defend,
But alas for Nelly's hopes and scheming,
She suddenly awoke – she had just been dreaming.

    Alison Halley
    Age: 11

There was a boy called Marcus Snoop
Who always, always, slurped his soup.
He slurped and slurped and slurped all day,
And in a most disgusting way.
He drove his mum and dad quite wild,
This nasty, horrid, slurping child.
They told him this, they told him that,
But nothing seemed to stop this brat.
One day his grandma came to tea
Her favourite son she'd come to see.

He told her of his son's delight
In slurping soup. That very night
She asked to see her grandson, who
Had nothing else at all to do.
"You really must stop slurping soup,
No one would think that you're a Snoop.
If you go on slurping your soup,
You won't look like young Marcus Snoop,
For you'll have turned into a pig,
With curly tail and snout so big."
But Marcus didn't really care,
He fidgeted and pulled his hair.
The next day poor young Marcus Snoop
Sat down and started slurping soup.
But straight away his nose grew big
And Marcus Snoop is now a pig.
So now all you who slurp your soup
Remember poor young Marcus Snoop.

    Elizabeth Stoodley
    Age: 12

A do-it-yourselfer, Molly Crab
Thought her décor very drab.
So into town she went one day
And bought some paper, bright and gay.
Ready pasted, easy strip,
It really was a worthwhile trip.
Her husband said with quite a snap,
"I can't do such things with my bad back."
So left to work alone was she,
And worked away contentedly.
She didn't know she had damp walls
"Bill, look just how this paper falls!" she shrieked.
So entered Bill through papered door
And likewise ceiling, walls and floor
Were also scenes of gay profusion
And, amidst the mad confusion,
Bill in horror gaped around
Then, to his amazement found
Struggling underneath a mat,
Their pasty, papered little cat.
"Ah, diddums," gently whispered Bill,
"You've made poor pussy look quite ill."
But pussy had had quite enough,
She couldn't stand the ghastly stuff.
She leaped around from wall to wall
And did her best to tear down all.
"She's gone quite mad, she's gone insane,
My room will never look the same!"
But still the pussy would not stop
So Molly chased her with a mop.
Down came paper, down came plaster

Total chaos and disaster,
But left on the wall they found
All sorts of panels, square and round.
With more uncovered it proved to be
From the time of King Henry.
They then sold this for quite a price
And now the décor's very nice.
Just as it had been meant to be,
But this time done professionally.

Carl Marshall
Age: 15

This is an ode to my friend Nellie,
Who couldn't sit to watch the telly,
The reason was a painful spot
Which came in a place where it ought not.
She asked her mum, so old and wise,
What was the cause of this demise.
Her mum said, "Don't eat chocs and sweet
When watching Lesley, John and Pete.
Chips and fries will give you pimples
As well as growing fattening dimples!
So my advice to eat with care,
Instead of toffee, munch a pear.
Your teeth will also be quite white,
If you remember to clean at night."
So Nellie did as her mum said,
Ate fruit and cheese instead of bread.
Now she has skin so soft to feel
That spots are just no longer real.
So now she sits to watch Blue Peter
Eating an apple and nothing sweeter.
So if you've spots and can't watch telly,
Go on a diet like my friend Nellie.

Judith Lloyd-Williams
Age: 11

I've written this to Lucy Lark,
Once famed for singing in the park,
She used to trill with the big brass band
Her swirling tambourine in hand
The people used to gather round,
Astounded by her high-pitched sound,
And half the village population
Marvelled at her weird gyration.
Beginning with a daring twirl,
The tambourine began to whirl;
Down to the ground, up to the trees
Over her shoulder and up through her knees,
The flute it whistled, the tuba boomed.
For Lucy Lark was sadly doomed,
And as the crowd began to shout,
Her set of new false teeth flew out!
Disaster struck, a fearful twang,
The notes got higher as she sang,
The local priest, a Mr Vickers,
Cried, "Oh, my Gosh, there goes her knickers!"
The consequence was rather drastic,
She changed her name to Lucy Lastic!

Alison Green
Age: 11

When Fred was small, his father said:
"Young man, it's time you went to bed,
You look quite tired it seems to me,
And after all, it's best to be,
Early to bed an' early to rise,
So's you'll be 'ealthy, wealthy an' wise!"
So off went Fred, in tragic tones,
Emitting the most fearful groans,
He hates to go to bed, you see,
In fact, he's just like you or me!

But when he'd brushed his pearly teeth
And imitated Edward Heath,
He changed from brush to flannel red,
And washed his neck and ears and head.
Then thinking, with exceptional glee
"I'll 'ave a short sharp bath," said he.
So, filling the bath like a castle moat,
He went to fetch his plastic boat.
The tap still running, foolish Fred,
He should have turned it off instead!
But being stupid, Fred rushed out;
It overflowed, without a doubt!
And spilled onto the lino floor,
Then seeping out beneath the door,
It flowed along to Freddie's room,
Where little Fred was sunk in gloom:
He couldn't find his boat at all,
The plastic one with funnels tall.
Not seeing water coming in,
It covered him from toe to chin,
Poor Fred tried swimming with all his might,
But sadly, 'twas a tragic night!
Young Fred was drowned, as you can guess;
The bedroom floor was such a mess!
The moral is, without a doubt,
Don't leave taps running: TURN THEM OUT!

Alison Vale
Age: 12

There was a lad named Adolphus Elfinstone,
Who never could leave birds' eggs alone,
He would climb up to the highest nest
So's he could have the biggest and best.
Spotted, plain, big and small
Name an egg, he had them all.
His mother would plead and implore in vain:
"Adolphus, don't steal eggs again,
Or all our birds will emigrate
And that, I'm sure, even you would hate."
But, Adolphus did not heed this warning
And very early one Sunday morning
He went in search of a great big eagle
Knowing, of course, that it was illegal.
And paying no heed to the KEEP OUT signs
And the threats of very expensive fines,
He walked bravely through the sanctuary gates
Equipped with all his eagle baits.
He spied this bird upon a rock
Guarding its eggs all round the clock.
It cast a dirty look at the traitor,
As though to say "I'll deal with you later."
Master Elfinstone walked up to this bird
And said very politely, "Madam I have heard
You have the most delightful eggs,
Could I please have one?" he daringly begs.
The eagle does not say a word
(Which is really quite natural for a bird)
She just swoops down upon the lad
And dear, oh dear, his ending was sad.
This heartless eagle ate every bone

Of our daring young Elfinstone.
The moral, surely you have guessed,
Free-range hen's eggs are the best.

Alice Oxholm
Age: 14

This is the tale of Percy Procket
Who thought he'd like to build a rocket.
He found some tins and bits of string,
And started to invent the thing.
As he worked hard in the garden,
His mother cried, "I beg your pardon,
Are you going to the moon?"
And promptly fell into a swoon.

"Oh, no," Perce said, "let's make it Venus,
I think we'll manage it between us."
Then all the family climbed aboard,
Perce lit the fuse and up they roared.
Dad looked around and checked their course,
Then started tapping things in morse.
They whizzed past Jupiter and Mars
And several other famous stars
His mother shrieked in consternation,
"Let's try another constellation!"
Then Percy yelled, "That looks a big 'un,"
And landed them in Central Wigan.
A man in blue said, "What's this 'ere?
You've been an' gone an' smashed the pier."
Now Percy wails, "I know my place,
I've had enough of outer space.
It isn't for the likes of us.
I'll try a number seven bus."
Now, chugging past the Isle of Thanet,
He dreams it's some far distant planet.
Whilst driving with due care and "cartion"
Pretends the traffic lights a Martian.

Pauline Woodburn
Age: 14

This is the tale of Henry Crun
Who thought he'd have a bit of fun,
He bought some paint of brightest yellow,
This happy conscientious fellow.
He painted window sill and wall
And even painted ceilings tall.
On seeing this, said Mrs Crun,
"Lor', luv a duck! Wot 'ave you done?
I knew you meant to smarten up,
Looks like a bloomin' buttercup!"
On kneeling down behind the door
Henry started the lounge floor,
And reaching soon the farthest wall
Found himself on island small
In a sea of gayest yellow,
This silly, conscientious fellow.
"Help," he cried, "I'm in a fix,
It feels like 'Desert Island Discs',
Allow me now to make my choices
Of eight different discs and voices."
The moral of this tale is clear
Dear viewers of Blue Peter here,
Whenever painting on the floor,
Start with your back towards the door.

Jenny McFarlane
Age: 11

"Help," he cried, "I'm in a fix"

This is the tale of Bertram Spraggot,
Whose nose was eaten by a maggot.
The offending beastie – very rare,
Ensconsed itself inside a pear;
And in the act of crawling out
It penetrated Bertram's snout.
Conscious of this alien creature
Quickly devouring his facial feature,
The offending larva he tried to prick
With the aid of a sharpened cocktail stick.
He noticed then, with apprehension
His nose was smaller in dimension.
And as the minutes ticked away
He realised with great dismay,
Before that day was out, he doubtless
Would find himself extremely snoutless.
Picture poor Bertram, and shed a tear,
As he watched his proboscis disappear
Then Bertram felt the urge to sneeze –
The maggot dropped between his knees,
And then with a triumphant hoot
He squashed it underneath his foot.
Now Bertram has a hooter plastic,
Held on by very strong elastic.

Fiona Gemmell
Age: 15

This is the tale of Barbara Bait,
Whose hair was fine and rather straight,
The colour of it was plain and mousey,
And mother said, "Your hair is lousy."
So one day in a fit of wrath,
She took the shears and cut it off,
Which made poor Barbara rather sad,
She thought she looked just like a lad.
So mother said, "Don't be so surly,
Let's see what you will look like curly."
And Barbara screamed and howled and squirmed,
But mother said, "You'll have it permed!"
So in the chair she had to sit,
Then mother made a hash of it,
It was short and tight and frizzy
And everyone was in a tizzy
Barbara said, "I feel a fool,
They'll all laugh at me at school."
So off she went to school in tears
But all the kids allayed her fears,
For after all her sobs of passion
She found out she was in the fashion
For she was not the only one –
Everyone had had it done!

> Sara Bromby
> Age: 11

This is the tale of Brenda Bloggs,
Who always wore enormous clogs
One day when standing in the square,
A policeman said: "You can't park there."
"That parking space is booked for us,"
Said the crew of a passing bus.
As poor Brenda turned around,
She knocked three road signs to the ground,
"Oh dear," she said, "I do feel rotten,
My way home I've quite forgotten!"
"I'll take you home," the copper told her,
And place his hand upon her shoulder,
One clog fell off whilst in the park,
A young boy said: "Look! Noah's Ark!"
"Oh no it ain't," said a passing harrier,
"It looks more like an aircraft carrier,"
At this poor Brenda bared her feet,
And left her clogs out in the street,
No more can folks hear Brenda walking,
The way she creeps, is more like stalking,
She's happy now she has posh shoes,
And no more does she sing the blues,
Down the street no more clip-clops,
'Cos Brenda now is top of the pops.

> Lyn Jackson
> Age: 11

She knocked three road signs to the ground

This is the story of poor Amanda
Whose favourite pet was a cuddly panda.
It's name was Bill, and I've heard it said,
It had its own four-poster bed.
Amanda loved this panda dearly,
But one day it ate her, well nearly.
It lived on rice and curry powder,
And every day its voice grew louder.
All the neighbours quaked with fear,
When Bill the panda got too near.

Amanda was a scatty girl,
One day her head got in a twirl.
Instead of feeding ferocious Bill,
She watched Chelsea win two-nil,
Now Bill his stomach began to rumble,
How he'd love some apple crumble!
Crumble being in short supply,
Perhaps Amanda he would try
He pounced on her, did Bill the panda
And nearly ate up poor Amanda.
But her mother, just in time,
Said, "Come on gal it's five to nine,
It's time that you're in bed my one,"
Bill didn't half have an empty tum.
In desperation he ate his bed,
In the morning he was dead.
And that was the end of poor old Bill
All 'cos Chelsea won two-nil!

    Joslin Sanders
    Age: 13

This is the tale of Granny Rike
Who bought herself a motor bike.
This dear old lady of ninety-four,
Through the streets of town would roar,
With string bag flying in the breeze
Doing a ton with blissful ease.
Her children's kids cried, "Look at that,
Our Granny is a real cool cat!"
At parking meters she was fine
She always got away on time.
Our Gran one day met a dreadful fate,
At a disco session, stayed too late,
Like Cinderella at the ball,

Heard midnight striking in the hall –
Her platform soles clutched in her hand,
She galloped down the staircase grand,
Leapt upon her trusty steed,
Let in the clutch, set off at speed.
Arriving soon at the old folks' home,
Forgot to brake and landed on her dome,
"Oh, deary me," she sadly cried,
"There must be a safer way to ride!"
And now our Gran goes here and there
In a power-driven rocking chair.

Paul Sykes
Age: 11

This is the tale of Maggie Nutty
Who stuck her hand in a bowl of putty,
"Oh," she cried, "it does feel soft,"
And promptly cast it up aloft.
There it stuck upon the ceiling
Looking like the plaster peeling,
"Poke it down," poor Maggie said,
"Before it drops on someone's head."
Her husband leapt to Maggie's aid
But for his chivalry he has paid,
For where his toupee used to be
Stuck for all the world to see,
A thick brown cake of putty lies
Right down his forehead to his eyes.
Now Maggie's husband doesn't need a hat
Nor combs or anything like that,
Of going bald, he has no fear
He simply paints it twice a year.

> Jane Wyckham
> Age: 14